AF270368

Rain Forest Life

Purpose of the Rain Forest

by Julie Murray

Dash!
LEVELED READERS
An Imprint of Abdo Zoom • abdobooks.com

Level 1 – Beginning
Short and simple sentences with familiar words or patterns for children who are beginning to understand how letters and sounds go together.

Level 2 – Emerging
Longer words and sentences with more complex language patterns for readers who are practicing common words and letter sounds.

Level 3 – Transitional
More developed language and vocabulary for readers who are becoming more independent.

abdobooks.com

Published by Abdo Zoom, a division of ABDO, PO Box 398166, Minneapolis, Minnesota 55439. Copyright © 2023 by Abdo Consulting Group, Inc. International copyrights reserved in all countries. No part of this book may be reproduced in any form without written permission from the publisher. Dash!™ is a trademark and logo of Abdo Zoom.

Printed in the United States of America, North Mankato, Minnesota.
102022
012023

Photo Credits: Getty Images, Shutterstock
Production Contributors: Kenny Abdo, Jennie Forsberg, Grace Hansen, John Hansen
Design Contributors: Candice Keimig, Neil Klinepier

Library of Congress Control Number: 2022937231

Publisher's Cataloging in Publication Data

Names: Murray, Julie, author.
Title: Purpose of the rain forest / by Julie Murray
Description: Minneapolis, Minnesota : Abdo Zoom, 2023 | Series: Rain forest life | Includes online resources and index.
Identifiers: ISBN 9781098280123 (lib. bdg.) | ISBN 9781098280659 (ebook) | ISBN 9781098280956 (Read-to-Me ebook)
Subjects: LCSH: Forests and forestry--Juvenile literature. | Rain forests--Juvenile literature. | Temperate rain forest ecology--Juvenile literature. | Biotic communities--Juvenile literature.
Classification: DDC 577.34--dc23

Table of Contents

Purpose of the Rain Forest

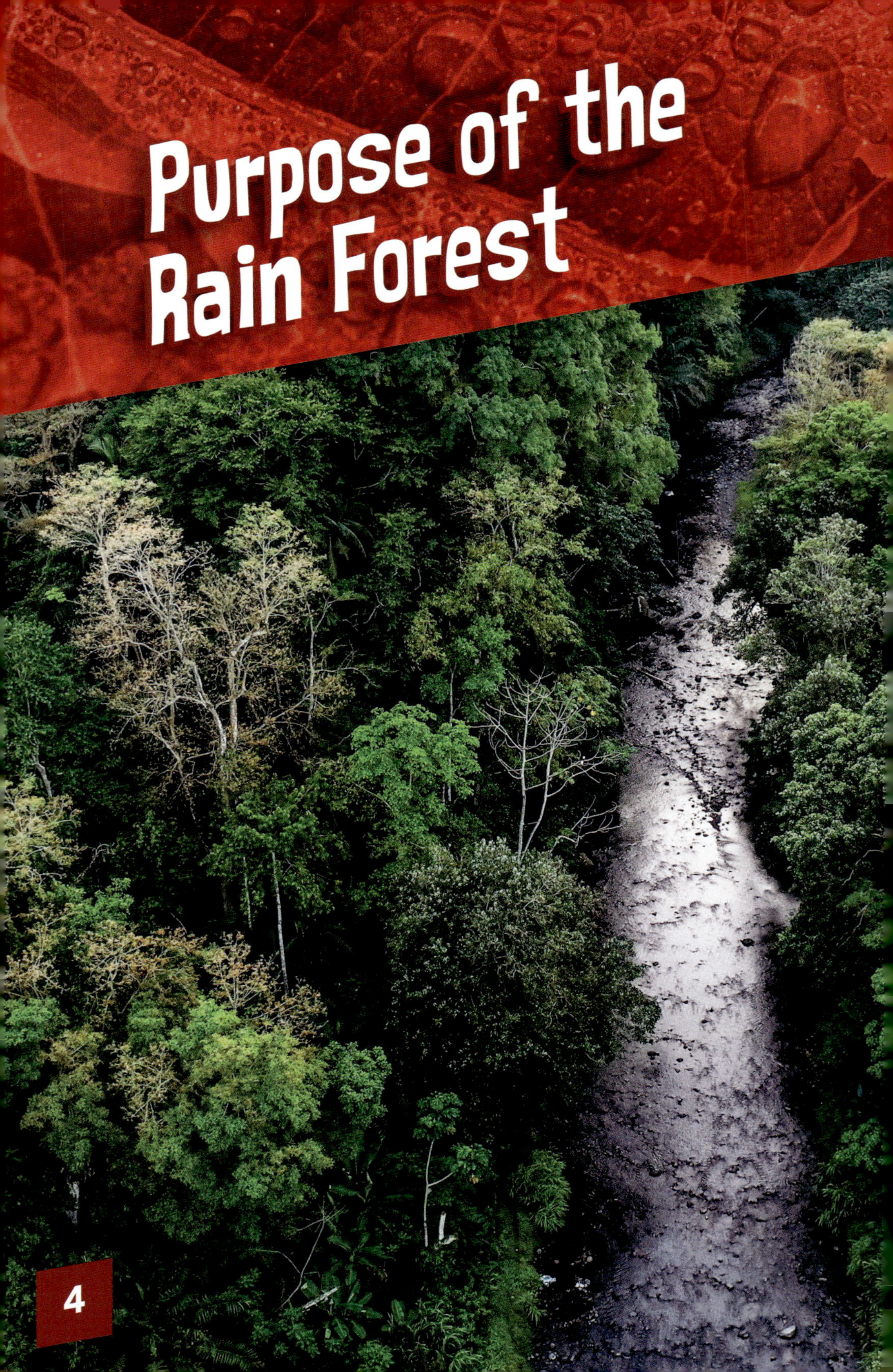

Rain forests are the oldest **ecosystems** on the planet. Some are more than 70 million years old!

Rain forests are important to all life on Earth. Half of the world's kinds of plants and animals live in and depend on rain forests.

What Rain Forests Provide

Rain forests provide a home for animals. Spider monkeys live high in the trees.

The plants provide food
for the animals. Macaws
eat seeds and nuts.

Rain forests help **regulate** the weather. They absorb and release moisture into the air. This keeps rain forests warm and **humid**.

Cacao fruit

Many things we use come from rain forests. Chocolate is made from the seeds of cacao fruit.

Some rain forest plants provide medicine. The bark of the cinchona tree has been used to treat **malaria** for more than 350 years.

Roots of plants in the rain forest prevent **erosion**. Without roots, soil would wash away.

Rain forest plants provide
clean air too! They absorb
carbon dioxide and
release oxygen.

- Rain forests are found on every continent except Antarctica.

- The Amazon rainforest may be home to more than 30 million people. They depend on the Amazon for food, shelter, clothing, and medicine.

- Rain forests play an important role in preventing **climate change**.

Glossary

carbon dioxide – a gas without color or odor that is made up of carbon and oxygen.

climate change – a significant and long-lasting change in the Earth's climate and weather patterns.

ecosystem – a community of living things, together with their environment.

erosion – the process by which the surface of the earth is worn away by the action of water, wind, or other natural forces.

humid – having a high amount of water vapor; damp.

malaria – a serious disease carried by mosquitoes that causes chills, fever, and sweating.

regulate – to control or adjust.

Index

Online Resources

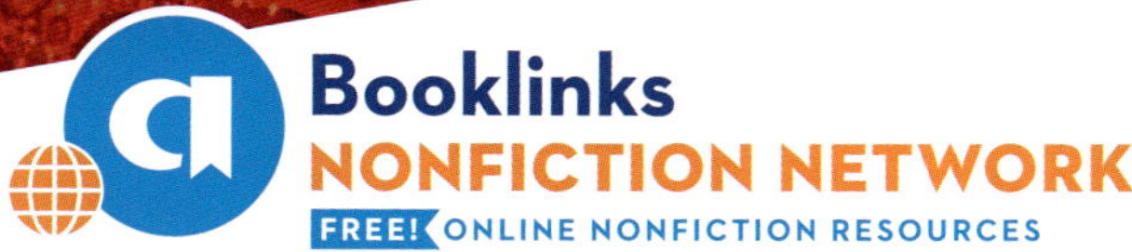

To learn more about the purpose of the rain forest, please visit **abdobooklinks.com** or scan this QR code. These links are routinely monitored and updated to provide the most current information available.